RAISED BED

THE ORG

By

Pauline M. Pears

First Edition, 1983.

 ISBN 0 905343 09 3

Printed by A. G. Bishop & Sons Ltd., Orpington, Kent.

Drawings by Nicky Scott

Henry Doubleday Research Association,
Convent Lane, Bocking, Braintree, Essex, CM7 6RW.

CONTENTS

FOREWORD
by Geoff Hamilton
Gardening journalist and broadcaster

In some respects gardening and farming techniques have come full circle.

Time was, before the advent of "artificial" fertilisers and pesticides, that gardeners and farmers relied for their plant nutrients and their pest control on purely organic compounds.

Farms were always mixed, with animals as well as food crops, so there was a plentiful supply of farmyard manure to recycle onto the fields. And there was always enough left over to supply local gardeners and allotments. Thus was provided a humus-rich soil structure and enough plant food to sustain quite acceptable yields of vegetables, grain and fruit.

Pest and disease control relied largely on natural predators and, because these enemies of plant pests were not themselves poisoned by chemicals, a balance was maintained.

Then science took a hand, first with the introduction of balanced artificial fertilisers, then with chemical pesticides and weedkillers. Quite suddenly, farmers began to increase their yields dramatically and gardeners grew flowers and vegetables like they never had before.

Pests and diseases became less of a problem too. A regular spraying programme banished the common pests from field and garden. Certainly a few eventually found a resistance to the chemicals and survived, but newer, more powerful chemicals replaced the older ones just as quickly.

No further proof was needed that the organic age was dead.

It is only now that farmers, gardeners and yes, scientists too, are beginning to realise the catastrophic effects of this wanton destruction of Nature's balance.

What we perhaps hadn't realised was that our soils were blessed with an inherent fertility arising from hundreds of years of careful husbandry. Since farming and horticulture began, we had always put back as much as or more than we took out. Only now is that fertility beginning to decrease. As recently as 1982 scientists at Luddington Research Station suddenly noticed that their soil was completely worm-free. With all the life-giving humus gone, plus the daily dose of chemical poisons, they could no longer survive to continue their vital work.

And pests and diseases are now on the increase too. It is a fact that, since the introduction of artificial pesticides, which have indiscriminately killed off natural predators as well as pests, the problems have never been greater. There is no doubt in my mind that you can only play around with Nature's balance for so long.

I am convinced that the future of farming and gardening, to say nothing of our own health, depends upon a rapid return to more natural methods of husbandry.

Of course we must learn by our mistakes and we must use much of the valuable knowledge we have gained along the way. There is no reason, though, why we shouldn't feed our plants organically and naturally.

Of course we must control pests and diseases, but if we do so at the expense of their natural predators we are laying up trouble for ourselves.

There is no doubt that enlightened farmers and gardeners are beginning to see the truth and it is with sincere enthusiasm that I welcome these books produced by the Henry Doubleday Research Association in conjunction with Clavering Organics. Read and digest well and help put a smile back on Mother Nature's face.

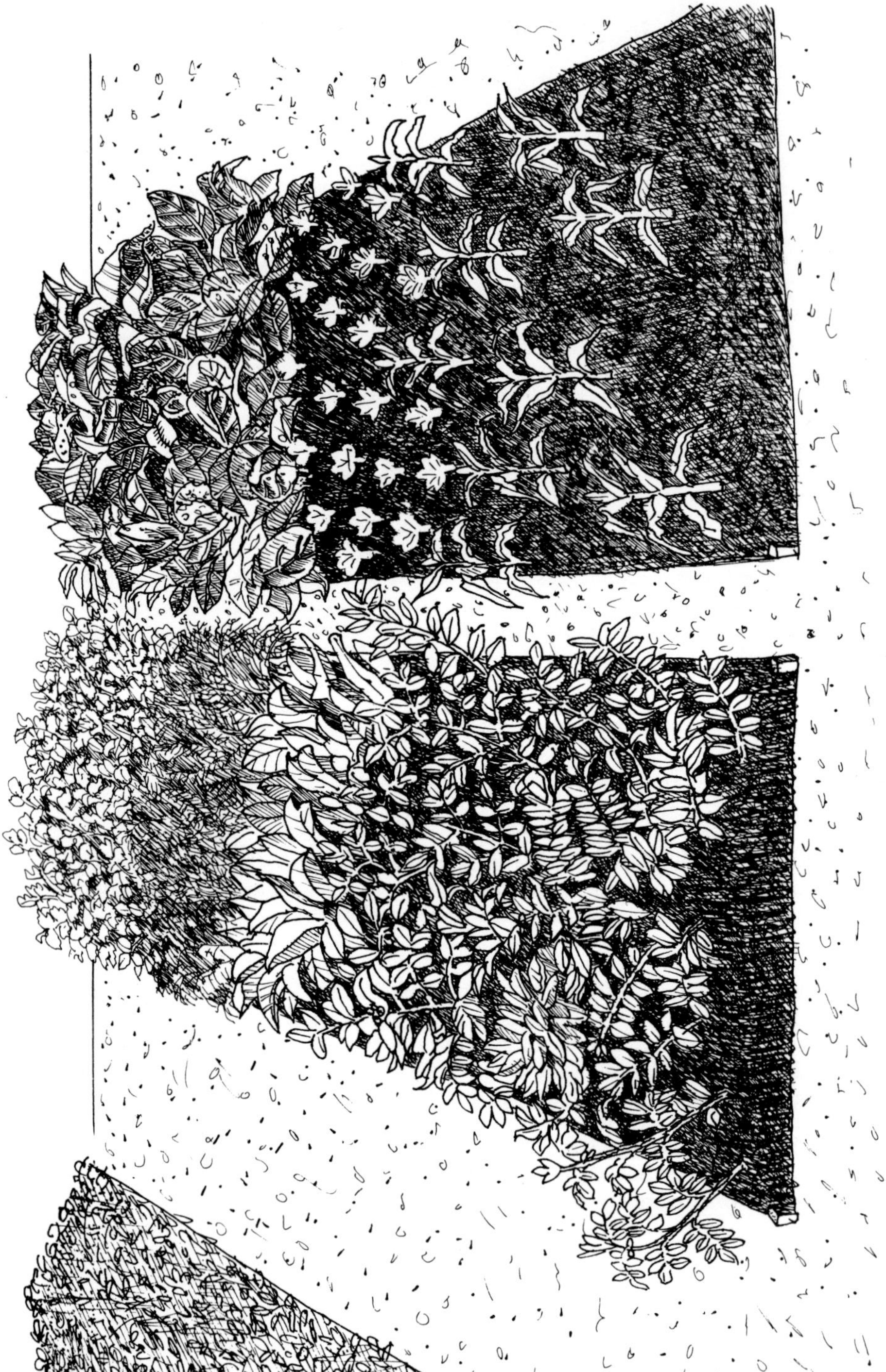

WHAT IS INTENSIVE RAISED BED GARDENING?

The 'Bed System' of gardening is a system of growing vegetables in which the garden is divided up into narrow beds (1.2 – 1.4 m wide) which are separated by narrow paths.

These beds can be 'raised' as a result of deep digging and incorporating organic matter. They stay raised above the level of the surrounding paths because they are never walked on, all work being carried out from the paths. Because the soil is deeply dug these are sometimes known as deep beds.

It is also possible to raise beds by building a wooden frame round a bed and adding extra soil and organic matter, and these could be cropped in the same way as the raised beds described in this booklet.

The beds are called 'Intensive' because the whole bed is very intensively planted; crops are grown at close spacing with each plant an equal distance from the others around it. This gives a much higher plant density than a 'conventional' system where rows are widely spaced.

Intensive Raised Bed Gardening is much older than our present day conventional system, which only evolved when vegetables began to be grown on a field scale, with crops sown in widely spaced rows to allow the passage of a horse-drawn hoe for weed control. This wide spacing gave higher yields, but only because of the weed control obtained. On a smaller scale where hand weeding is possible the Intensive Raised Beds can produce much higher yields.

The methods and ideas expressed in this booklet are, in the main, based on the experience of the Henry Doubleday Research Association, where an intensive raised bed system of gardening has been used and modified over the past four years. We are not saying that this is the only way to garden on raised beds; this is our method that we have developed to suit our individual requirements.

This booklet is intended to introduce the concept of Intensive Raised Bed Gardening to vegetable growers; it is then up to each individual to experiment and modify the system, if necessary, to suit their own conditions and requirements.

WHY USE THE INTENSIVE RAISED BED METHOD?

1. **Higher yields from less space:** Today more and more people are gardening in less and less space. The Intensive Raised Bed system packs many more crops into a small area than a conventional system could, giving higher yields for the space used, even when the area of paths is taken into account.

2. **Waste less time and energy:** In a conventional garden system, the whole vegetable garden is dug over and manured/fertilised and then only part of it used to grow plants in — the rest is wasted space between rows which only grows weeds. This is a waste of plant foods applied. The space between the rows is often used as a pathway — this is a waste of digging. With the bed system only the growing bed is dug and manured; this is then intensively planted. The paths are not.

3. **More control over crop size:** When the beds are sown/planted all the plants of one crop are equidistant from each other. In many cases if this distance is increased (within limits) the maximum size of the individual plants will increase; if the spacing is decreased, the size of the individuals will decrease. Some people like small onions for example, others larger ones . . . this system can suit them both.

4. **Less work:** Once the beds are prepared, there is less maintenance work required. Only the bed area needs to be looked after, and very often weeds are smothered out by the closely spaced crop plants. Any weeds that do get through are easy to remove from the uncompacted soil.

5. **Earlier cropping:** Because the paths are permanent and the beds are not walked on this can mean that you can get on to the garden to start work early in the spring without worrying about compacting the soil by walking on it. The looser soil of the raised bed should also mean that it will be better drained and warm up more quickly in the spring. As the plants are closely spaced, growth of each one is limited, so crops may also finish earlier.

6. **No more muddy wellies:** If the paths between the beds are well made, it should be possible to go out and sow, plant, weed and harvest without getting wet or muddy feet.

PLANNING AN INTENSIVE RAISED BED GARDEN

If you are establishing a new vegetable garden, or converting an existing one to the Raised Bed system, it is essential to do some planning before you start. You will have to consider location and orientation of the beds and their dimensions — which will depend partly on the space available and partly on the cropping plan that you decide on. You will also have to decide on the width of the paths and what they are to be made of. Some advice on making these decisions is given below.

Location

It is not always possible to choose an ideal location for the vegetable patch, especially in a small garden; if possible however it should be open to as much sun and light as possible and not too close to trees and hedges (whose roots will be taking goodness from the soil). For the majority of crops some shelter from the prevailing wind is also beneficial.

Orientation

Ideally the beds should run with the long axis north/south, so that both sides of the bed get equal amounts of sunshine. It may not be possible to have them exactly north/south but try and align them as near to that as you can.

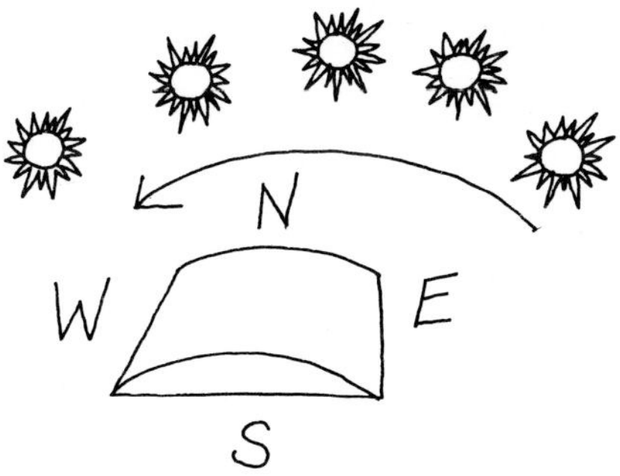

Right: All the bed receives sunshine.

Wrong: Half the bed is shaded.

Bed size

As the beds are never walked on it is obviously necessary to work from the surrounding paths all the time. This means the bed must be of a width to allow you to reach the middle comfortably from the path; 1.2m is a usual width though 1.4m is possible if you are taller and have longer arms. Any wider than this and it becomes very uncomfortable working the middle of the bed for any length of time. Narrower beds are possible but this increases the ratio of path to bed, making less use of the available space.

In theory the beds can be as long as you like, but it is often easier to manage the cropping with more smaller beds than fewer larger ones. This is something you will have to decide on while you are working out the cropping plan. Another factor to consider is that you should always walk round a bed to get to the other side. If the bed is too long it is very tempting to step across it which invariably means that the soil is stepped on. Long beds also mean that it is further to carry manure, compost, etc., from the main paths at either end unless you pair up the beds as suggested below.

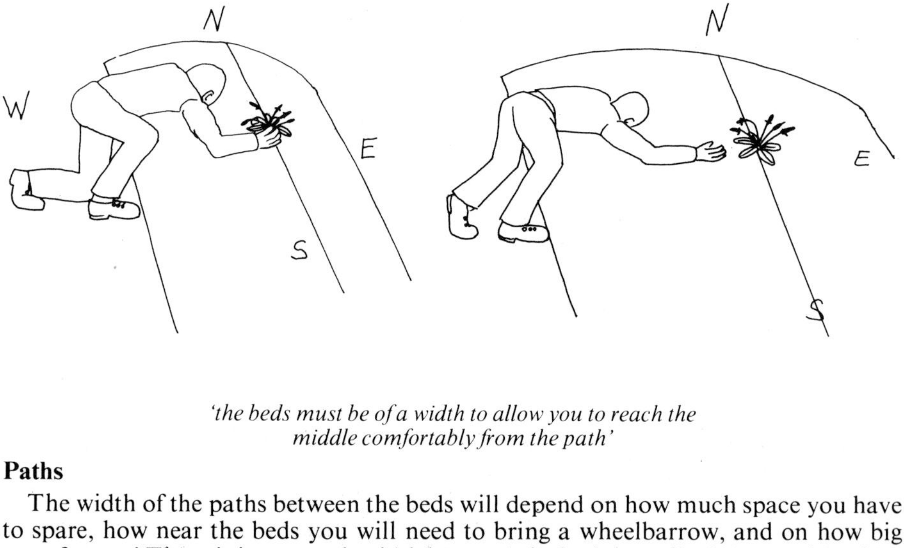

'the beds must be of a width to allow you to reach the middle comfortably from the path'

Paths

The width of the paths between the beds will depend on how much space you have to spare, how near the beds you will need to bring a wheelbarrow, and on how big your feet are! The minimum path width between the beds is really 450mm with wider paths at one or both ends to allow a barrow to be brought close. If you have larger feet a slightly wider path should be considered to prevent the edges of the beds being trampled. If space is not at a premium, it is more convenient to 'pair up' the beds, having a narrow path between them and a wide path between pairs so that a barrow can be taken the length of a bed, on the one side anyway

The paths can be made of sawdust, woodshavings, concrete, bricks, strips of carpet or just plain earth kept weed free. It is not really advisable to have grass paths as the grass will compete with the crops at least 150mm into the bed, and can reduce crop yields.

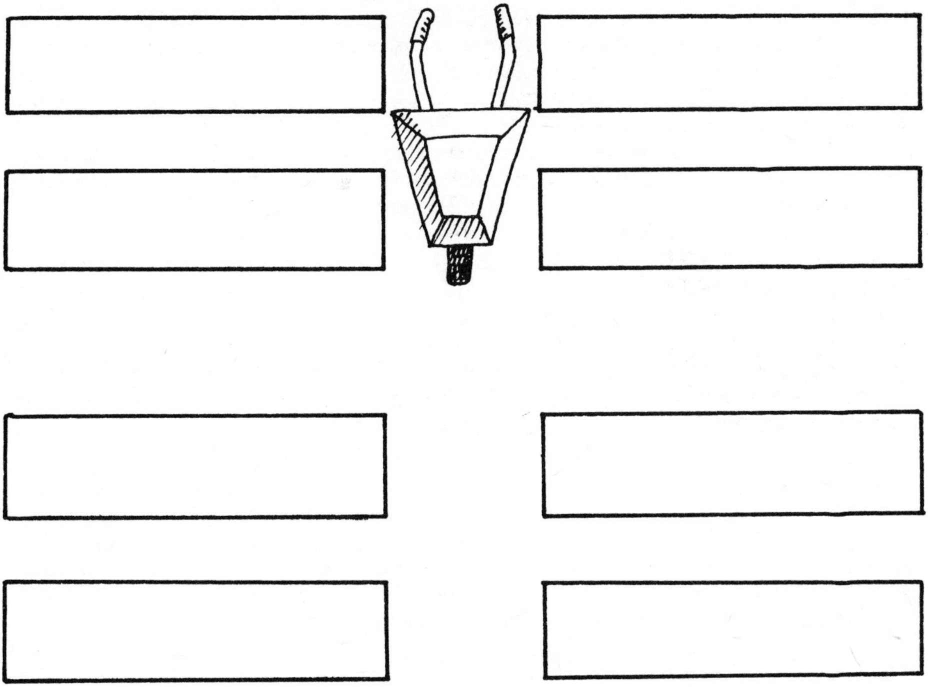

'a wider path between pairs of beds allows a wheelbarrow down the length of each bed'

Cropping

Planning the layout of the crops in an Intensive Raised Bed garden requires some thought, especially if you have not used this system of growing before. A rough outline at least should be decided on before you settle finally the size and number of beds to be made.

Ideally it is best to sow and plant up a whole bed at the same time; it is also best to completely empty each bed once a year so that it can be redug and shaped as necessary. This may mean re-organising your normal way of cropping slightly.

Firstly, work out approximately how much of each crop you require (either in number of plants or length of row) and calculate the area of bed that this will require (using the information given in the 'Crop by Crop' section). If you grow a large amount of any crop, such as potatoes, the layout is simple; that crop is given a whole bed (or beds) to itself. Where there are going to be several crops in one bed, try and group together those to be sown/planted at the same time of year. You could for example, have 'early spring' sown beds, 'late spring' sown beds, and 'after the last frost' beds. By juggling around the crops to follow on it is usually possible to empty each bed completely once in the season; this does not have to be in the autumn or in the spring necessarily. For example, the early sown bed(s) would include parsnips, which are left in over-winter, so the rest of that bed can be used for other overwintering crops such as winter cabbage, sprouts etc. This would then be empty for redigging in the late spring of the following year.

As you juggle the crops around you should begin to see the size that the beds will need to be to suit your situation. They should really all be the same size, so that when crop rotation is practised there is room for each set of crops on every bed. It is not easy to use a conventional 3 or 4 course rotation with this particular system unless you grow large amounts of each type of vegetable. One can, however, follow the principles of the rotation; such as by not growing brassicas or potatoes on the same bed more than once in three or four years. (This is to prevent the build up of clubroot (of brassicas) and eelworm(of potatoes) in the soil). Remember also that if you lime the cabbage beds, potatoes should not be grown there for a couple of years.

When planning the layout of the crops on an individual bed, try and always put the taller crops at the north end of the bed to avoid shading the shorter ones. Do not put less vigorous crops (such as onions) next to more vigorous ones (such as carrots), or the one will smother the other and reduce the yields at the edges of the block. Either put the same sort of crops next to each other, or leave adequate space between them. If it seems clear that you may want to dig a bed before it is empty (which may be the case where overwintering crops such as leeks or spring cabbage are involved) put these long term crops at one end of the bed, or digging will be impossible.

An example of a cropping system on Intensive Raised Beds is given opposite. There are 8 raised beds, each 1.2m × 3m though they are treated in some cases as if they were four beds of 1.2m × 6m. Remember that this is only one example and that each person with their own individual requirements will come up with a different plan. Don't worry if you don't get it right at first; it is much easier to see what will work and what won't once you have the system going.

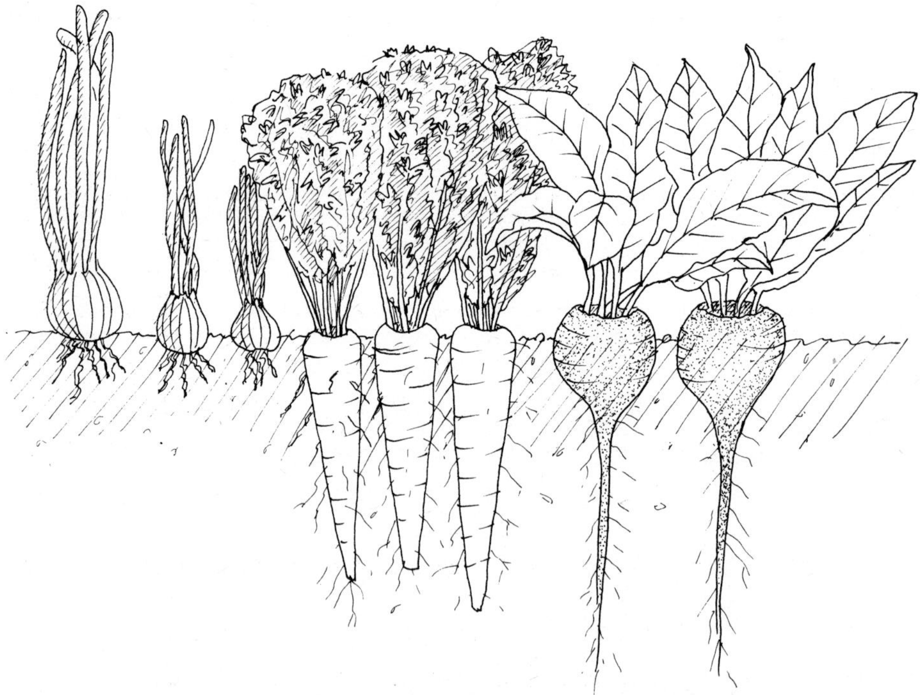

'do not put vigorous crops close to slower growing ones'

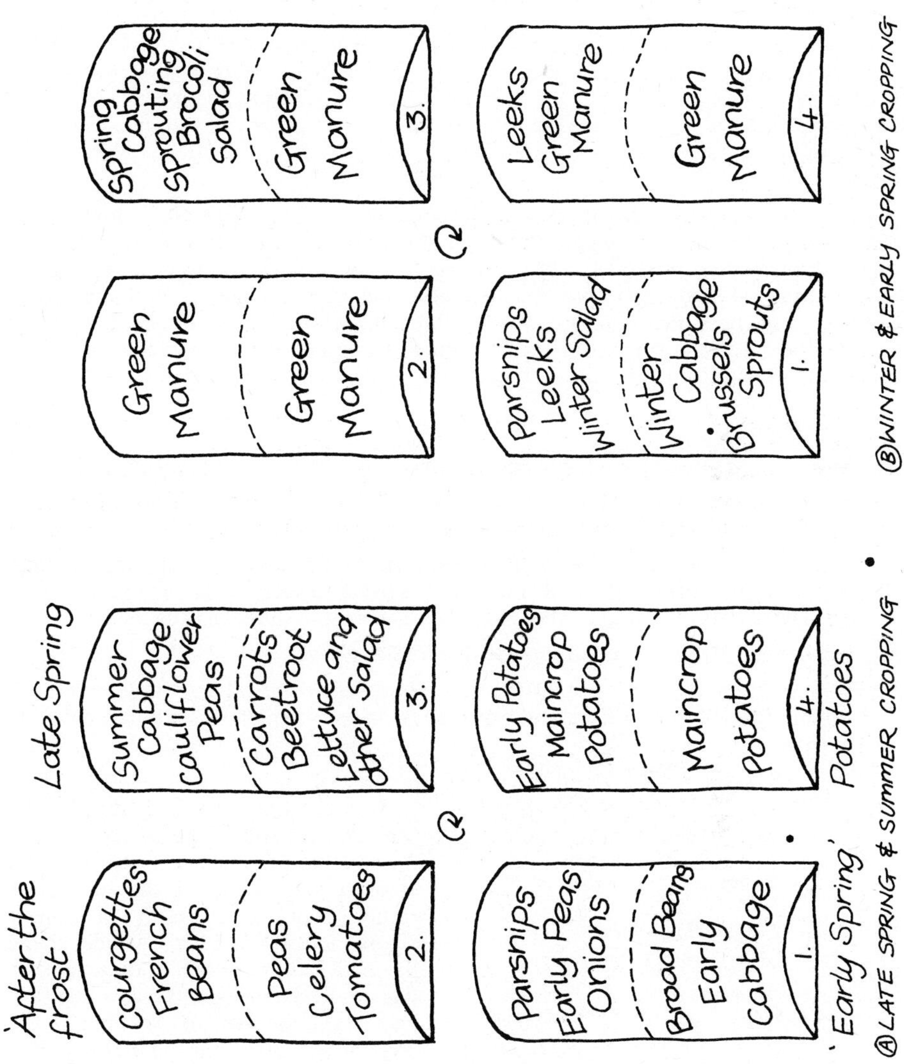

One Example of a Cropping Plan for Four Intensive Raised Beds.

Notes :
1. The crops move on one bed each year in a clockwise direction.
2. If clubroot is a problem each bed can be divided along the middle to make 8 separate hall beds. In this case the rotation is exactly as before (the crops from two half beds staying together), but after 4 years the crops change ends.

PREPARING THE BEDS

First season

It was mentioned earlier that Intensive Raised Beds are raised partly as a result of 'double digging'. This process is not always essential but it is a good initial soil preparation, making sure that there is not a 'pan' preventing adequate drainage or rooting; it also helps to remove the more pernicious weeds. If you feel, however, that your soil is already adequately dug, move on to the next section. ('Subsequent Seasons').

In the first season then, mark out the area of each bed with sticks and string, making sure it is 'square', and then double dig each one as outlined below. 'Double digging' means that the soil is disturbed two spits (spade depths) deep. If your soil is very compacted it may be impossible to dig that deep the first season; in that case just dig as deep as possible, increasing the depth each season. This is the one time when you will have to walk on the bed, so to minimise compaction it is advisable to stand on a board or similar while you are digging.

Double Digging

1. Dig a trench one spit wide and one spit deep; put the soil into a wheelbarrow.
2. Stick a fork into the soil of the 'second spit' below, and move it backwards and forwards to loosen the soil; do this across the width of the bed.
3. Dig out the next top spit, placing the soil in the first trench. If the soil changes colour in the depth of the first spit be very careful to keep the layers the right way up. This can take practice. Make sure you dig right to the edge of each bed.
4. Loosen the soil of the second spit with a fork as above.
5. Repeat 2 and 3 to the end of the bed. Here you will find you have an empty trench; this is filled with the soil from the first trench which was put in the wheelbarrow.

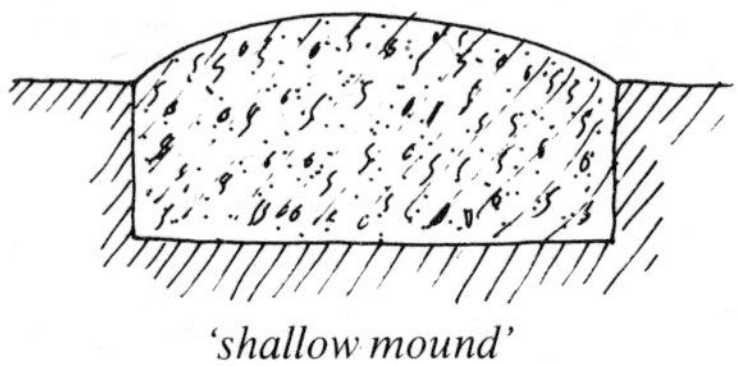

'shallow mound'

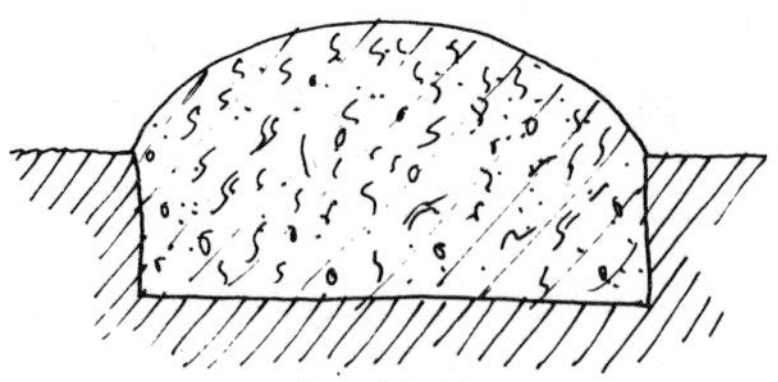

'too high'

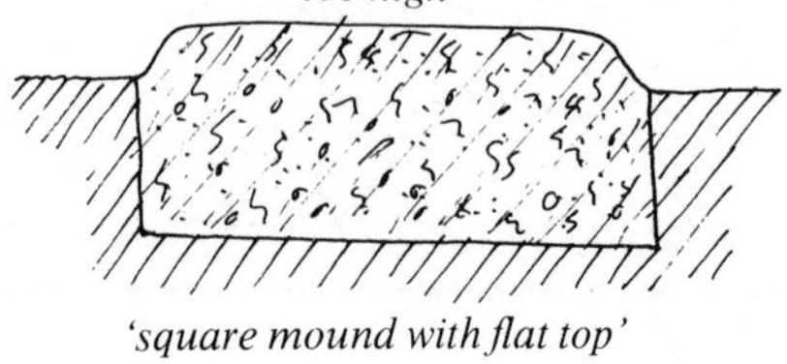

'square mound with flat top'

After digging, rake the bed to form a shallow mound. The sides of the mound should not be too steep or else erosion will occur. If the mound is rather high, as a result of double digging a heavy soil for example, shape the bed into a squarer mound with a flat top. Rake the soil to give a fine tilth and plant as soon as possible. After digging you may find the bed is higher at one end than the other; in this case rake some soil back to the lower end before finally shaping the mound.

Each bed need only be double dug once a season. After crops are harvested and before new ones are planted during the year the bed need only be lightly forked and raked back into shape.

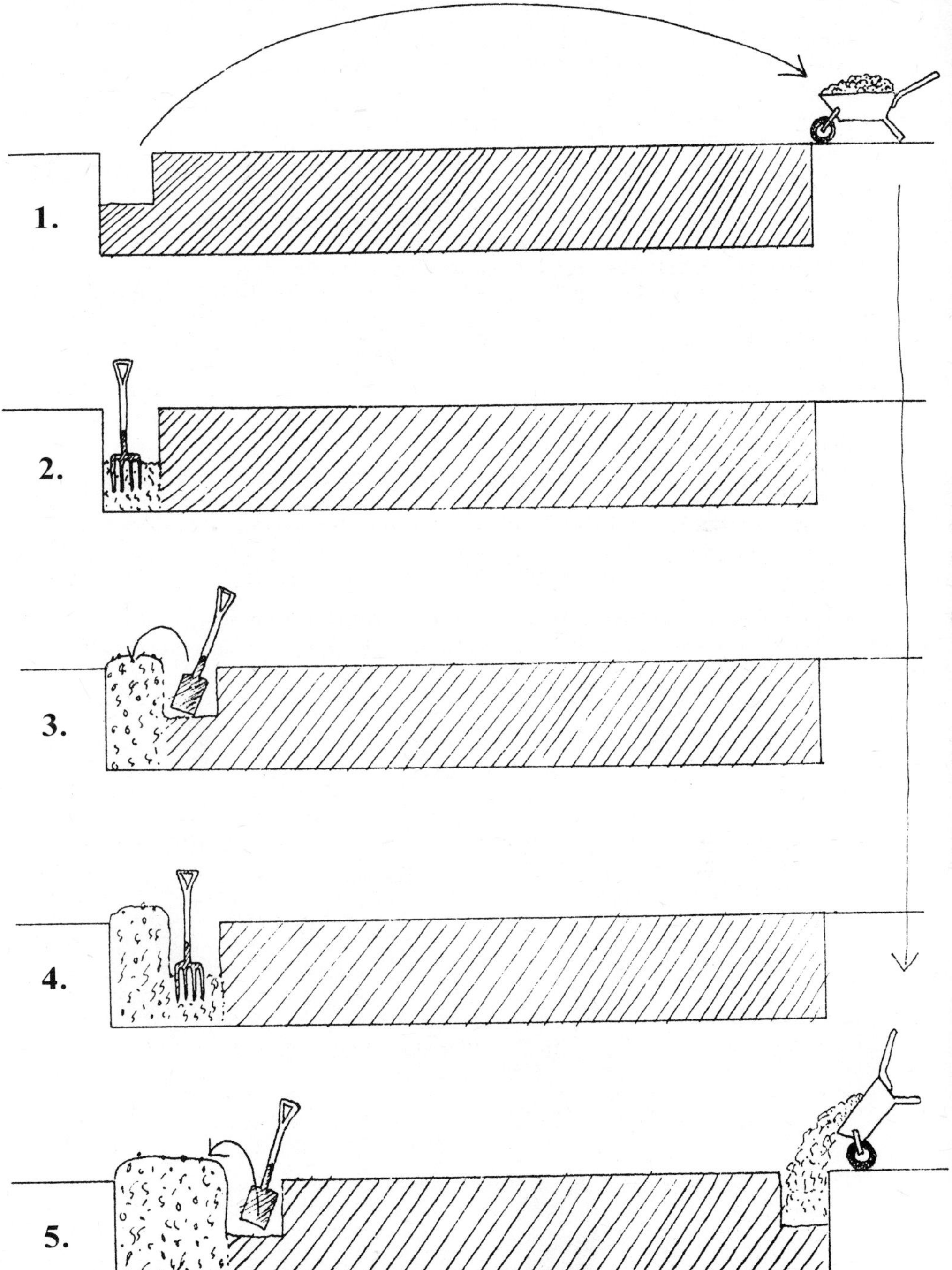

'double digging'

Subsequent Seasons

After the first year of cropping there are several alternative treatments for the beds.

If in the previous year the soil was difficult to dig and two spits deep was impossible to achieve, it would be advisable to repeat the double digging for as many seasons as it takes to achieve two spits of loose friable soil.

If the soil was well dug in the previous year it should not be necessary to loosen the second spit again; the bed can then just have a 'single dig' using a board to stand on as before. This digging can be used to incorporate bulky organic manure and compost.

If the top layer of soil is still light and friable the bed can just be forked over to reshape it and to incorporate any organic fertilisers or lime.

After digging etc the bed should be reshaped as before. As the soil is never walked on, compaction should not be a problem, but the soil will gradually settle and the beds become flatter and flatter. A double digging once every few years would raise them again.

Timing the Digging

The soil should not be dug when it is either very wet or very dry as this will damage the structure. If the soil is very heavy and tends to be slow to drain and warm up in the spring, it may be best to do the main digging in the autumn when the soil is at a workable moisture. In the spring it will then only need forking over and shaping. The beds could also be dug in the summer, after early crops have finished and before the next crop is sown or planted.

With a light soil the beds can be dug whenever they become empty. If the soil is very dry the beds can be soaked with water and left for a day or two before digging.

'mulch the surface between widely spaced plants'

MANURING AND FERTILISING

Vegetables grown intensively on raised beds need the same kind of organic fertilisers and manures as any others, but it is probably wise to increase the amounts used by a quarter to a half as much again. The benefit of using organic fertilisers is that it is much more difficult to 'overfeed' the plants, as you are feeding the plant via the soil system rather than directly. Nutrients not taken up by the plant will remain in the soil system for use by following crops.

Bulky manures, such as well rotted farmyard manure, homemade compost or proprietary brands of packaged manure should be spread over the surface of the bed before double digging, single digging or whatever, and incorporated as the soil is cultivated. These bulky manures supply nutrients and also organic matter, which helps condition the soil and increase its water holding capacity. This can be very important especially on light land as an intensively planted bed uses a great deal of water. If possible, additional quantities of organic matter in the form of leaf mould or, as a last resort, peat, can be added to further increase water holding capacity. If required, organic fertilisers such as hoof and horn (for slow release nitrogen), blood, fish and bone (a good general fertiliser), rock phosphate and rock potash should be sprinkled over the surface after the double digging and lightly forked in. Lime is applied in the same way.

Apart from seaweed meal, it is advisable to apply manures/fertilisers in the spring rather than the autumn to prevent the rain washing soluble nutrients out of the soil. Whether you do an autumn or a spring application, try not to leave the soil bare overwinter. The best idea is to sow a 'green manure' crop if no vegetables are being grown. These are fast growing crops such as grazing rye, winter tares and field beans which take up nutrients from the soil as they grow through the winter; these nutrients are then released when the plants are dug in the next spring and broken down by the bacteria.

In the growing season most of the surface of the bed is covered in foliage; with the more widely spaced crops (e.g. cabbage, tomatoes) this is not the case though, so either plant small crops in between or mulch the ground with materials such as compost, leaf mould or comfrey leaves. Comfrey leaves will also supply potassium to the soil as they decompose, so they are especially beneficial for tomatoes.

CROP SPACING

On an Intensive Raised Bed System crops are laid out in 'blocks',

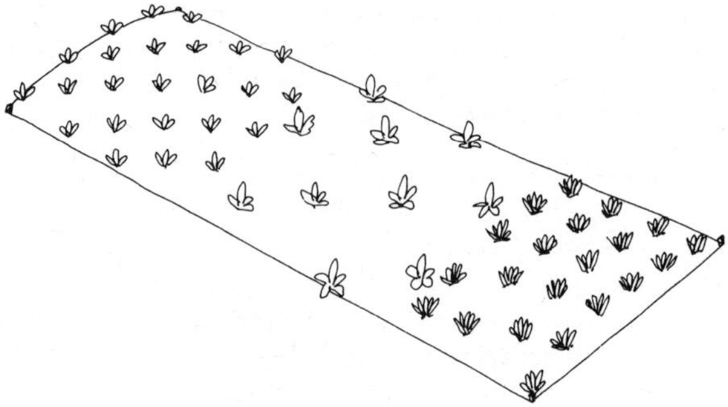

with each plant equidistant from all the others of the same crop around it, rather than in the more conventional widely spaced rows.

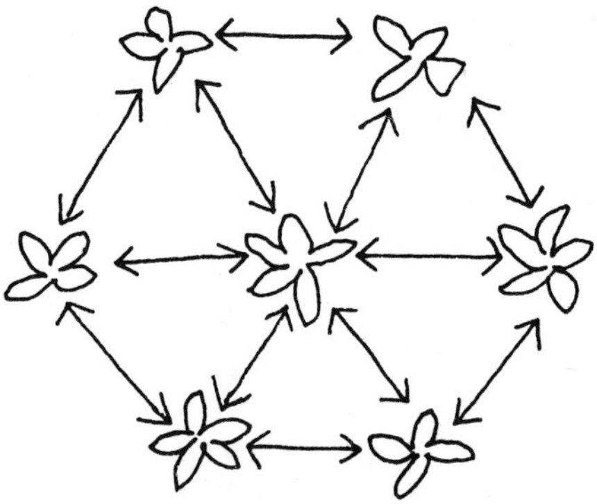

The plants are 'staggered' to make best use of the space. This means very intensive planting, which can give considerably higher yields than a conventional layout.

This equidistant spacing of the plants also means that it is simple to control the individual plant size, just by altering the distance between plants. Onions, for example, at a spacing of 225mm will give very large bulbs; at 100mm spacing, on the other hand, individual bulbs will be smaller but total yields will be higher. Smaller bulbs will store for longer periods and are often more useful in cooking. There are limits to how far the spacing can be adjusted; if it is too wide yields will decrease as the plants cannot grow large enough to fill the space, if too close the total amount of plant matter may be very high but the actual part you want to eat may be almost non-existent.

Suggested spacings are given in the Table, on page 19, but the optimum spacing for the individual gardener will depend on the size of vegetables required, and the soil fertility. Adjust the distances to suit. You will find that only a single figure is given; this is the distance between plants every way. If you plant in rows across the bed the rows can be slightly closer together to take account of the 'staggered' planting. This will make maximum use of the space.

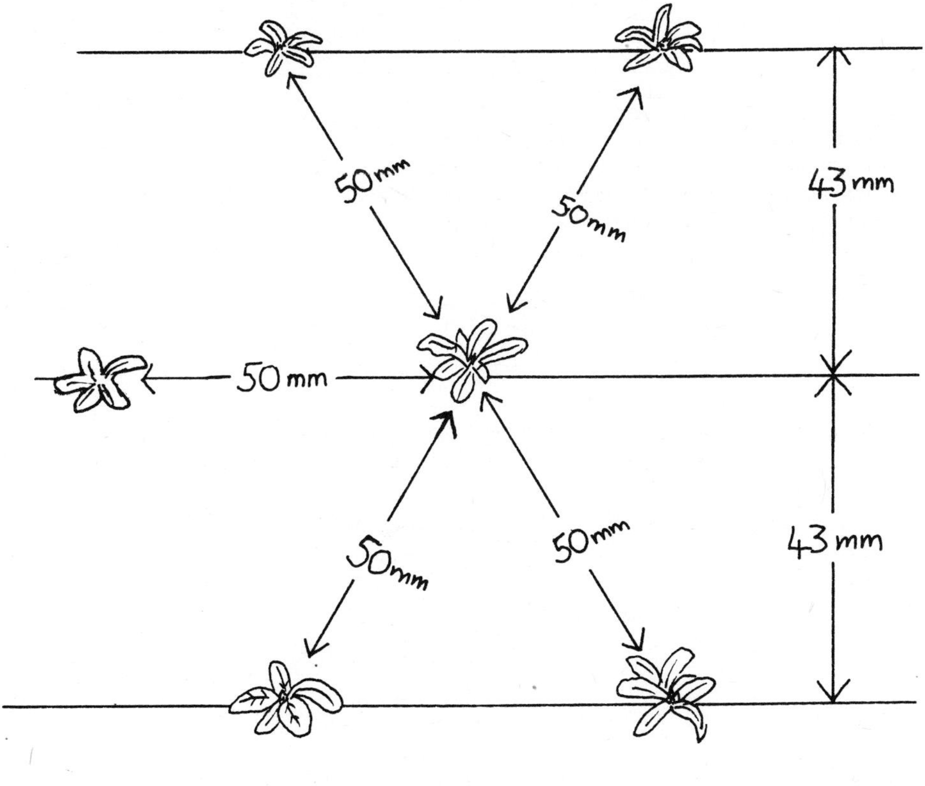

'the rows can be slightly closer together than the between-plant spacing'

Where a crop is not mentioned, try out the spacing suggested on the packet for between the plants, within the row.

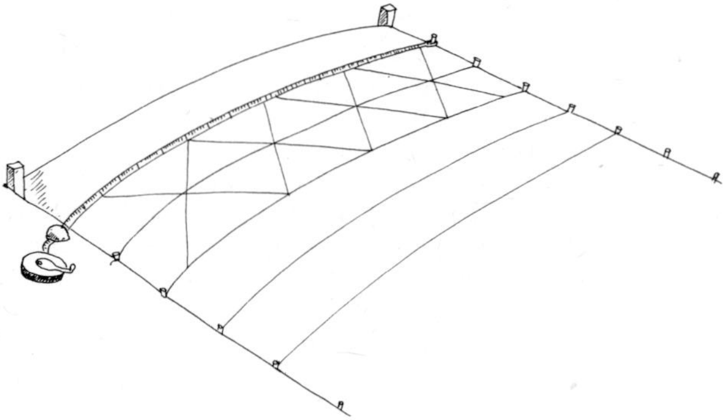

'mark the position of each row with a stick and measure each individual spacing'

It is important to plant out/sow the crop as accurately as possible to make maximum use of the close spacing. A board marked with distances, or a tape measure is essential. The most accurate way is to mark the position of each row with a stick either side of the bed and measure each individual spacing. Less time consuming is to measure accurately every second row and plant by eye the intervening row.

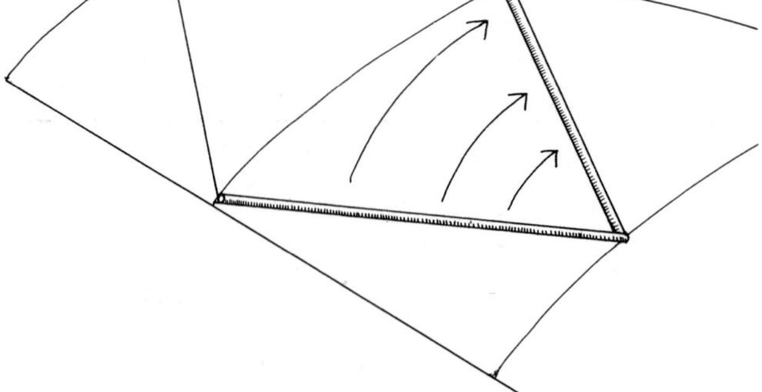

Once you get used to it you can use a stick, cut to the between-plant spacing, to measure distances once the first row has been accurately measured. It is a good idea to check every so often that the rows are still 'square' across the bed. When sowing seed, either station sow at precise spacings or sprinkle thinly in rows and thin to required spacing. You will notice that some crops are still quite widely spaced; the space between these plants can be used for quick intercrops such as radish, lettuce, spring onions, as long as they don't interfere with the main crop.

SOWING AND PLANTING DISTANCES — CROP by CROP

Beans		**Leeks**	75 — 225mm
Broad, dwarf	225 — 300mm	**Lettuce**	
Broad, tall	150 — 225mm	Heading	225mm
French, dwarf (fresh)	225 — 300mm	Leaf	225mm
dwarf (dry)	100mm	Cut & Come Again	25 × 125mm
Beetroot		**Onions**	
Early	50mm	Bulb	100 — 150mm
Maincrop	75 — 150mm	Salad	25mm
Brussels Sprouts	500 — 750mm	**Parsnips**	75 — 150mm
Cabbage		**Peas**	
Chinese	225 — 300mm	Early	75mm
Autumn & Winter	450 — 600mm	Maincrop	100mm
Spring	225 — 300mm	**Potatoes**	
Summer	250 — 450mm	Early	225mm
Carrots		Maincrop	300mm
Early	up to 125mm	**Sweet Corn**	375mm
Maincrop	75 — 100mm	**Tomatoes** (Outdoor)	
Celery	250mm	Tall	525 — 600mm
Courgettes	600mm	Bush	450mm
Cucumber	600mm		

Notes (i) The figures given indicate suggested spacings between plants in all directions, which is why there is often only one figure.
(ii) Where two figures are given, the smaller one will give smaller plants, the larger one larger.
(iii) See 'Crop by Crop' for more details.
(iv) Spacing between rows will be slightly closer than between plants.

BEETROOT

Early Beet

Can be sown direct in March/April, in a band across the bed with approximately 50mm between seeds. The roots are picked small at first, which leaves more room for the others to grow larger.

This crop can also be sown earlier in the greenhouse for transplanting. The seed is sown in small pots or peat blocks so that the roots are not disturbed at transplanting. The use of 'multi-sowing' reduces the number of blocks required; each block is sown with 2 seeds (which are really clusters of seeds), and 4 or 5 seedlings are allowed to grow. The blocks are planted out at 300mm spacing, and the beet shoulder each other out of the way as they grow.

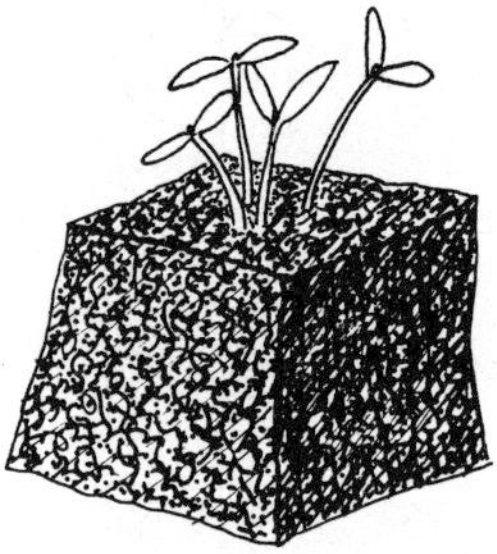

Maincrop Beet

This is sown later in the season, after the last frost, at 75mm, to give a medium sized beet. They can be thinned out as you pick for eating so that some grow larger, but small beet are by far the sweetest.

BROAD BEANS

Dwarf Varieties

These are the easiest to deal with on the bed system. They grow about 300mm tall and produce several stems. Sow any time from early spring to midsummer, at a spacing of 225mm or 300mm depending on the variety (see seed packet for details). They need no support.

Tall Varieties

These can be grown in double rows across the bed with spacing of 150mm in the double row and 460 — 600mm between the double rows. More in keeping with the system, they can also be grown in a 900mm wide band across the bed, with a 225mm staggered spacing between the plants. Both ways the plants will need staking to keep them up. Remember to plant a tall crop like this at the north end of a bed so that it does not shade the other crops.

'the plants will need staking to keep them up'

BRUSSELS SPROUTS

If they are planted too close together you will get lots of plant but very few sprouts. A spacing of 500mm (minimum) should give a good crop, with the sprouts tending to be ready to pick all at the same time, which can be ideal if you want to freeze them. A wider spacing of 610mm to 750mm should give a longer cropping season. The plants are raised in a greenhouse or in a seed bed elsewhere and planted out when the land is available. It is advisable to press down the soil well round the plants, and also to stake them if the soil is light to prevent them rocking in the wind, as this can cause the sprouts to 'blow'. The Brussels can be interplanted with lettuce, for example, to use up the space.

CABBAGE

Spring Varieties

Plants should be raised in a seedbed or boxes and planted out as usual. They can be spaced at 225 or 300mm and gradually thinned for eating so that the later ones end up at 300mm. As the crop overwinters it should go in an 'overwintering' bed, or at least be planted at the end of a bed so that it does not get in the way when preparing the bed for planting the following spring.

Summer Varieties

These can be grown at a wide range of spacings, depending on the size of cabbage that you require. A spacing of 250 — 300mm will give small heads of any variety and there are also specific varieties such as Hispi and Minicole which are designed to grow at such spacings.

For larger heads, plant out at 450mm.

Autumn and Winter Varieties

Plant out at 450 — 600mm each way.

CARROTS

These are an ideal crop to grow on the bed system; they appreciate the deeply dug soil and give a very good foliage cover that smothers the majority of weeds.

Early Carrots

These can be sown from February onwards, sprinkled as thinly as possible in wide drills. They can then be pulled from pencil size onward, leaving some to grow larger. To get the quickest crop of decent-sized early carrots, though, they should be given plenty of space to grow, sown at 125mm spacing. The easiest way of doing this is either to sow a pinch of seed every 125mm, or to sow rows 125mm apart across the bed and then thin to 125mm within the row as soon as the seedlings are big enough.

Maincrop Carrots

These can be sown from March onwards, waiting till late May/June to sow for storage. Spacing should be about 75 — 100mm each way. The seed can be sown as above, either 'station sown' at the required spacing, or sown in rows and then thinned to the right distance.

CELERY

Self-blanching celery is the easiest to grow, and it is usually recommended that this be grown in blocks anyway as this aids the blanching. Plants should be raised indoors, preferably in peat blocks or divided polystyrene trays, and kept growing steadily; any check to growth will encourage bolting. Plant out, after all danger of frost is past, into a well manured soil, at 250mm spacing. Keep the plants well watered, especially immediately after transplanting.

CHINESE CABBAGE

This crop is usually sown directly where it is to grow. Plants can, however, be transplanted when small if raised in peat blocks or small pots. If the roots are disturbed at transplanting the plants will tend to bolt. Some varieties can be sown in the spring; others are only suitable for growing when the day length is shortening (i.e. after mid-summer), otherwise they will bolt. The final spacing should be 225 — 300mm. Chinese cabbage is best grown quickly with no check to growth, so it must always be adequately supplied with water. The addition of organic matter to the soil, either dug in and/or as a surface mulch, which helps water retention in the soil, will benefit the crop. Otherwise regular watering is essential in dry periods.

COURGETTES, MARROWS AND CUCUMBERS (Outdoor)

These crops appreciate a well dug and manured soil. It is best to choose bush varieties of courgette and marrow so that one plant does not take over the bed, and to pinch out the tips of cucumbers if they trail too far. These crops would be best grouped together on one bed, or sharing with another vigorous crop. Raise seedlings in pots indoors or in the greenhouse and plant out at 600mm spacing. Alternatively, once the soil has warmed up (in early May or later) sow direct at 600mm with two or three seeds per 'station'. Cover with a cloche or polythene sheet to encourage germination and thin to one seedling.

FRENCH BEANS

Dwarf varieties for eating fresh

These beans can be sown as close as 100mm for the highest theoretical yields. Unfortunately this tends to make the plants tall and straggly so that they fall over. This makes harvesting difficult unless you use a yellow-podded variety (whose pods are easily seen), and also creates a perfect environment for slugs and snails. A spacing of 225mm or even 300mm is much more practical. The seed should not be sown until late April/early May (at the earliest) as it will not germinate well in a cold soil. Cover with polythene or a cloche to aid germination. Alternatively, raise plants in peat pots in frame or greenhouse for transplanting after the last frost.

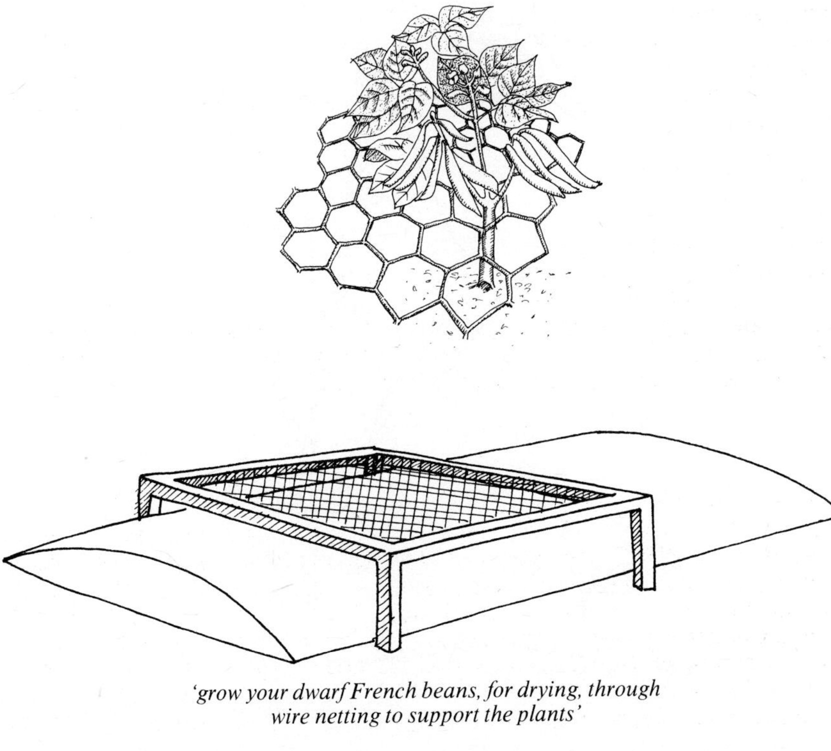

'grow your dwarf French beans, for drying, through wire netting to support the plants'

Dwarf varieties for eating dry

There are many varieties suitable such as Purley King, Chevrier vert, Brown Dutch. The plants for producing dry beans should not be picked fresh at all, to give the pods the maximum drying time. They can be sown at 100mm spacing (once the soil has warmed up) and then supported by a piece of wire netting stretched horizontally over the bed, about 225mm above the ground. When the pods are dry the whole thing is removed and the plants pulled out of the netting. (This could be done with beans for eating fresh but it would make picking more difficult). If the pods are not fully dry the netting and plants can be hung up together to finish drying.

LEEKS

Leeks can be sown from March to May, being planted out from June to early August. As they overwinter well it is advisable to plant them out on an 'overwintering' bed. The ultimate size of the leek depends on size at transplanting, the spacing, and the nutrient status of the soil. Planting out large plants into well manured soil (into dibber holes as usual) at a spacing of 225mm will give highest yields. The closest spacing recommended is 75mm which does give a lot of leek but each individual is very thin and obviously many more plants are required. Vary the spacing to suit your requirements.

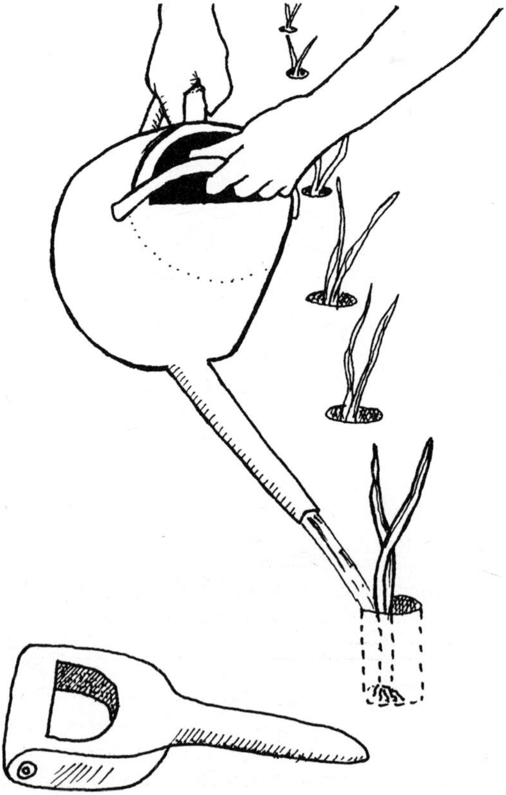

'plant leeks into dibber holes'

LETTUCE

Heading Lettuce

This is traditional lettuce with a heart. These should be planted out at a spacing of 225mm or sown in rows 225mm apart and gradually thinned to 225mm in the row.

Leaf Lettuce

This is a 'loose leaf' lettuce which does not form a solid heart. Individual leaves can be picked as required, and the plant left to grow on. Sow/plant as for heading lettuce.

Cut and Come Again Lettuce

This is a method of growing lettuce which is well suited to the bed system, giving high yields from a small area. The lettuce is sown in rows 125mm apart with approximately 25mm between seeds, and the plants are not thinned.

This encourages formation of leaves rather than hearts. As soon as the plants are tall enough to harvest (in 4-7 weeks), the leaves can be cut for eating, leaving a 25mm stump. The stumps are watered well and left to regrow another crop of leaves, which can be cut again later. This type of lettuce can be sown through the season from mid April to the end of August to give a supply of leaf lettuce from mid May to October, much more quickly than a conventional heading lettuce. Avon Crisp, Valmaine, Lobjoits Cos and Paris White Cos are suitable varieties for growing by this method; others may be bitter at the young stage at which they are harvested.

MIXED SALAD

This is a relatively new introduction into this country from Europe. Seed is sown broadcast from early spring. A range of salad plants come up — usually including rocket lettuce, purslane, chicory and others; these can be cut to give an instant mixed salad, and some will regrow. Some plants die out early and others appear to take their place, surviving the winter and ready to grow the next spring.

ONIONS

Spring Salad Onions

These make a good 'intercrop' between rows of widely spaced crops such as cabbage, tomatoes and broad beans. They can also be sown in a wide drill across the bed at about 25mm and picked as required.

Bulb Onions

These can be grown from sets or plants, planted out in the spring. A spacing of 100mm will give high yields of medium sized onions; increase the spacing up to 225mm to give larger individual bulbs. The only problem with the 100mm spacing is that it seems to make the plants more likely to be infected by mildew, presumably because there is less air movement around them. If this is a problem in your garden increase the spacing to 150mm.

PARSNIPS

Another crop where the size of the individual plant is easily controlled by spacing. Station sow (3 seeds/station) when the soil has warmed up slightly, as the seed is very slow to germinate. Spacing of 75— 150mm can be used, depending on the size of root you require and the fertility of the soil.

PEAS

Early Dwarf Varieties

These can be sown in a block spaced at 75mm and grown without support, as they only grow 300 — 450mm high.

'leafless peas'.

Maincrop Varieties

These generally need some kind of support, so sow them in triple rows across the bed, at 100mm spacing, with 300 — 450mm between the triple rows. These peas do not really suit the bed system well; much better are the so called 'leafless' or semi leafless varieties such as Bikini and Eaton. These are mainly stem and tendril with leaves very much reduced; sown in a block they support themselves well and the lack of leaves means that air and light penetrate the block.

POTATOES

It is a good idea to devote a whole bed (or several whole beds) to potatoes as the foliage is luxuriant and can quickly smother neighbouring crops. The bed should be well manured and the tubers planted out at a spacing of 225mm for early varieties, and 300mm for maincrop varieties, in trowel holes 150mm deep.

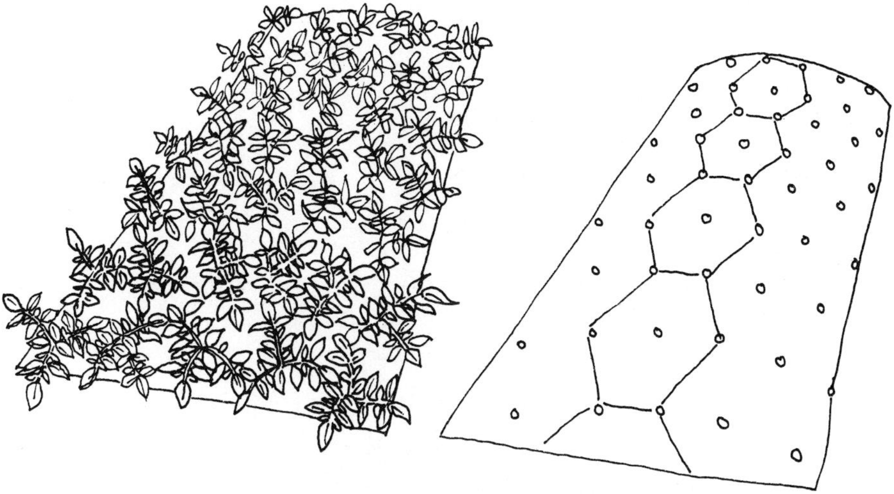

The shoots emerge very quickly through the light, well-dug soil, so make sure that they are not damaged by the frost; either plant a little later than usual or cover the early shoots with straw or leaves if frost is likely. The plants also grow extremely quickly with foliage soon covering the whole bed. It may be necessary to weed the crop once but the luxuriant foliage should suppress any subsequent weeds. At such a close spacing earthing up is not possible, but there does not seem to be a problem with green tubers. As the plants are so close each produces fewer tubers than usual so there is not the usual over-crowding that forces some tubers to the surface where they go green in the light. The close spacing also makes the haulms much taller than normal and they tend to flop over, and will overwhelm neighbouring beds if nothing is done. The foliage can be pruned to a certain extent and/or tied back with strings all round the bed.

The potatoes use large quantities of water, so increase water holding capacity of the soil with organic matter if necessary, and water in dry periods. The earlier start and the close spacing, which limits growth of individual plants, mean that the crop can finish a week or two earlier than a conventional one. Yields/sq.m. can be increased appreciably. Unfortunately the higher yields are only obtained at the expense of many more seed potatoes (65 times as many per square metre as a conventionally sown maincrop). To reduce the cost it is possible to cut tubers over 60g (2oz) in weight in half lengthways (making sure there are sprouts on both halves) just before planting, treating each half as a seed potato. This practice is not always recommended as the tubers may fail because of disease; this should not be a problem if you are careful only to cut healthy large tubers and anyway at such close spacing one or two missing tubers should be no problem. It is not a good idea to cut early potatoes if you want them early, as they rely on the food reserve in the tubers for fast early growth.

Care should be taken at harvesting so as not to damage too many tubers.

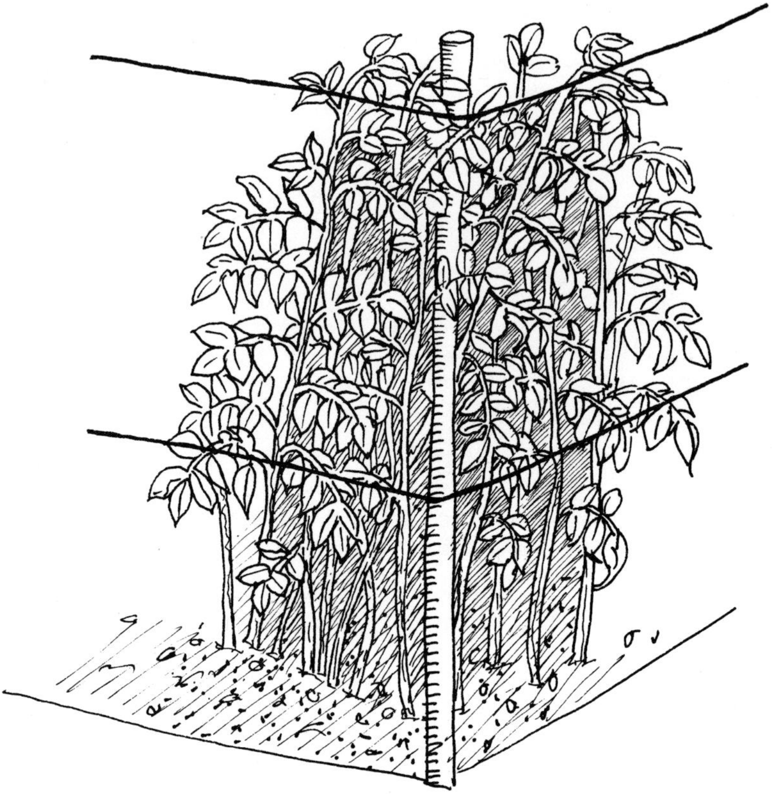

'potato foliage will need to be tied up'

SWEET CORN

This crop is always best grown in a block as this makes for more effective pollination. Reserve one whole bed for corn, or plant it at the northern end of a bed to prevent shading. The seeds can either be sown in pots in a frame or greenhouse and transplanted at 375mm as soon as danger of frost is past, or station sown directly into the bed at 375mm with two seeds per station. A covering of polythene will aid germination; remove it once the seedlings have emerged, or cut holes in the polythene and allow the plants to grow through. This will give an earlier crop, but remember that if it is clear polythene weeds can be a problem.

OUTDOOR TOMATOES

Tall Varieties

These can be planted out at a spacing of 525 — 600mm, depending on the variety. A large variety such as Gemini, for example, will need 600mm; Gardeners' Delight is a small plant, with smaller tomatoes, and can be planted at 525mm. The plants can be intercropped with lettuce to use the space.

Bush Varieties

e.g. Alfresco, Arla, Sleaford Abundance. These are a low-growing bushy type of tomato which are not staked and do not have the side shoots pinched out. The bed system suits them well as it is impossible to walk between rows of these plants unless very wide spacings are used. The seed can be sown in pots (pregerminated in a warm place if you do not have a greenhouse) with 3 seeds per pot, and all seedlings left to grow — they are not thinned. They are planted out from April under cloches and mid-May in the open, again without thinning. Using small pots with several plants restricts the growth of individual plants and makes cropping earlier. The spacing is 450mm each way.

The crop can also be sown directly into the bed. Pregerminated seed is fluid sown at 450mm spacing with 3 seeds/station. Again all the seedlings are left to grow. Seed can be sown under cloches from mid-April or in the open from late April. Whether direct sown or transplanted, an earlier crop can be obtained by allowing the plants to grow through a layer of polythene which remains on the soil surface.

Because the plants are so close and the fruit is on or very near the ground, there does tend to be a lot of nibbled or rotten fruit. Despite this yields can be extremely high and, if growth is restricted, early too.

RUNNER BEANS

Research has shown that the highest yields of these climbing runner beans that can

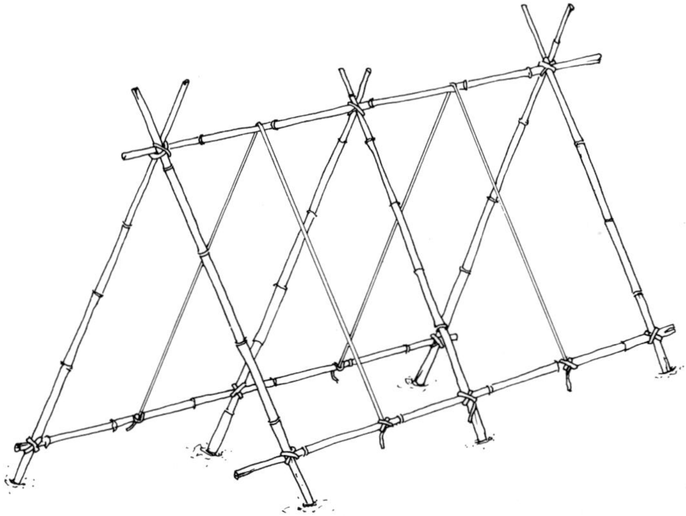

'strings can be stretched between alternate canes'

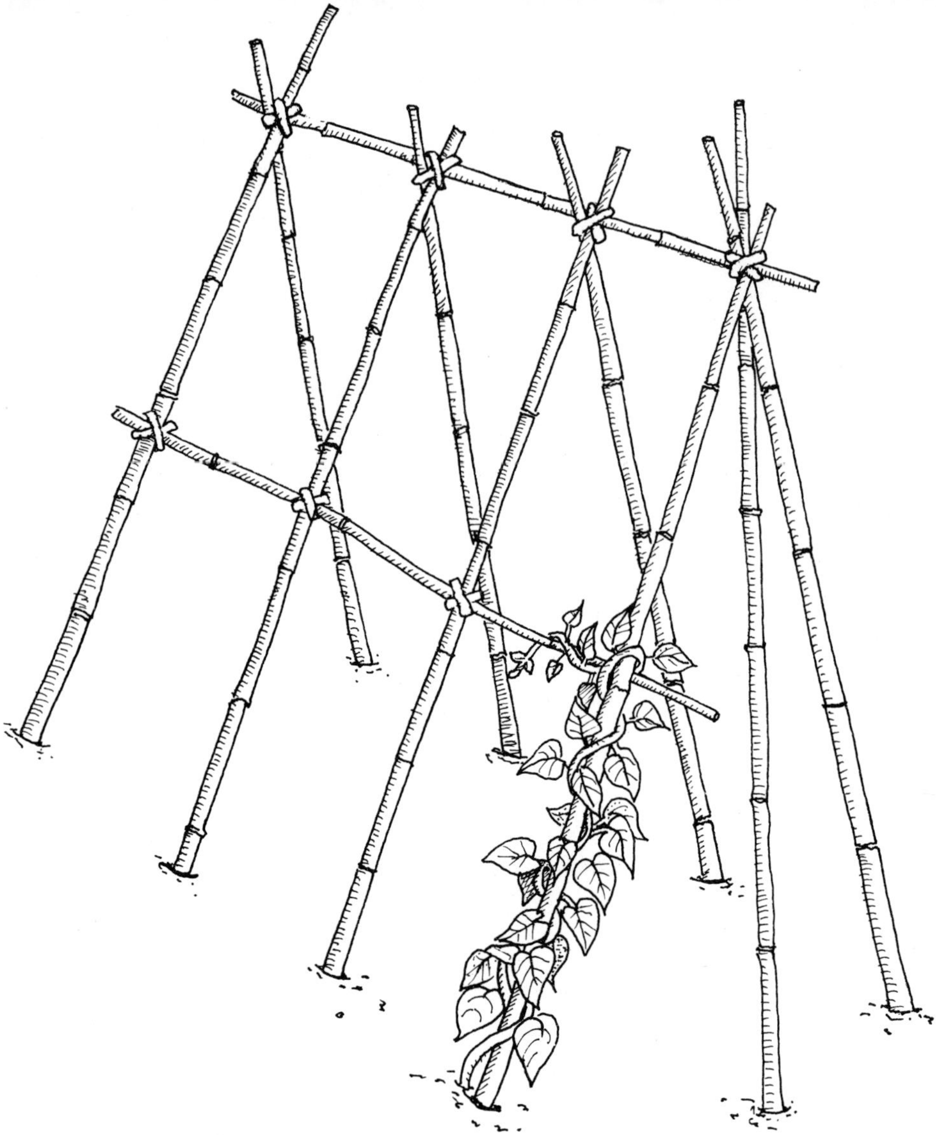
'each plant is grown up a cane'

be obtained on a bed system are achieved by growing plants in a double row — with 600mm between the two rows and 150mm between the plants. Each plant is grown up an individual cane. This does mean a large number of canes if one is used every 150mm; alternatively crossed canes can be placed every 600mm and strings stretched in between (as in the diagram on page 29).

If you only require a few runner beans they could be grown up a 'wigwam' structure at the end of one bed.

Climbing beans can of course always be grown without any support; in which case the tips are nipped out once they start to 'run'. Yields will not be as high, obviously, but the plants are said to crop earlier.

WEEDING

On the bed system most of the weeding has to be done by hand as the plants are too closely spaced to allow a hoe between. Because of the close spacing, however, you should find that one weeding is quite sufficient, with the foliage smothering any subsequent weeds; in fact with potatoes you may not need to weed at all. Onions are one closely spaced crop where regular weeding is required, as the leaves don't form a close cover and weed competition can reduce yields.

Hand weeding tends to be quicker on the bed system as the well dug soil makes it much easier to pull the weeds out.

PROTECTED CROPPING

It is always useful to be able to protect crops, both from animals and birds, and from the weather. Often the problem is that the cloches/frames we have don't fit exactly over the crops that have been planted. This problem need not arise on the raised beds, though, if standard-size frames/cloches are purchased, or made, to fit the whole width of the beds. This means that they can be moved from bed to bed and will always fit. Because the plants are so close together the space under the cloche/frame is used to its maximum.

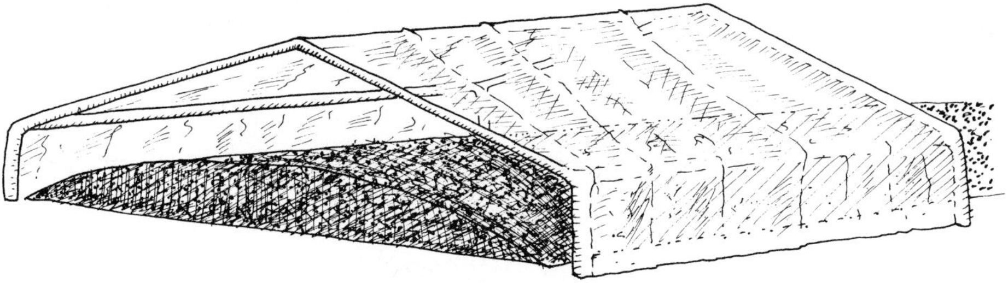

A polythene-covered frame/cloche can be purchased or made to fit across the bed. This can be used to extend cropping in the autumn, protect crops overwinter and in the early spring. If it is used to cover a prepared empty section of bed overwinter, sowing can start much earlier than usual in the spring.

A simpler frame covered in netting (simpler because it does not need to shed water) can be made to protect crops against birds, rabbits, cats, etc.

It has been found that a polythene barrier erected around carrots (like a roofless cloche) can substantially reduce damage from the carrot root fly. This method would be particularly economic on the bed system where there are so many roots in a small area. The barrier could be made simply with polythene stapled round four corner stakes hammered into the bed, or a sturdy permanent but movable barrier made for use year after year. Enclosing carrots in this way can also give higher yields, as it is like growing them in a 'mini greenhouse'.

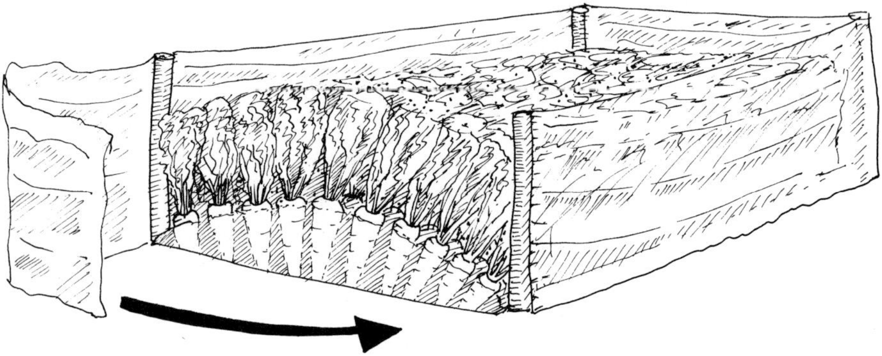

CONVERSION TABLE: MILLIMETRES TO INCHES

25mm	**= 1″**	**225mm**	**= 9″**
50mm	**= 2″**	**250mm**	**= 10″**
75mm	**= 3″**	**275mm**	**= 11″**
100mm	**= 4″**	**300mm**	**= 12″**
125mm	**= 5″**	**450mm**	**= 18″**
150mm	**= 6″**	**600mm**	**= 24″**
175mm	**= 7″**	**750mm**	**= 30″**
200mm	**= 8″**	**900mm**	**= 36″**

1000mm = m = 3′ 3″